KU-129-562

Contents

Foreword
Bishop John Kirby, Chairman of Trócaire

The eve of the Great Jubilee of the Year 2000 is a particularly appropriate time to refocus our attention on Christian inspiration behind the work of Trócaire and our sister organisation in England and Wales, CAFOD (Catholic Fund for Overseas Development). The founding documents of both organisations provide very clear mandates and situated these within the work of the Church and within Catholic social teaching.

No issue is more central to the work of Trócaire and CAFOD than food in our world. The huge numbers of people who lack access to food or the means to produce it, most of whom live in developing countries, is a challenge to us as Christians. As Pope John Paul II has emphasised: "A type of development which does not respect and promote human rights is not really worthy of humankind" (*Sollicitudo Rei Socialis 33*). One of the most basic human rights is the right to food and it is on this right that many others depend.

Previously titles in this series covering Human Rights, Famine and Land show the interconnectedness between issues and taken together with this new booklet by Josantony Joseph highlight that power imbalances and poverty are at the core of food insecurity in our world.

This series provides an important opportunity for Trócaire and CAFOD to invite eminent scholars to examine major strands in our work and to elucidate from a theological perspective the impulses that motivate the practical projects and programmes which our agencies support around the developing world. The result is a rich resource of analysis, reflection and restatement of the Christian commitment to solidarity and oneness of the human family.

We are particularly pleased to have Josantony Joseph as author of this booklet. Josantony as a dynamic Executive Secretary of the Asia Partnership for Human Development has been a partner and friend of both Trócaire and CAFOD. I would like to puy tribute to him for contributing so generously of his talent, energy and time in the preparation ot this reflection. Trócaire and CAFOD owe to our series editor, Professor Enda McDonagh, a profound gratitude for the inspiring guidance he has shown to authors and agency staff engaged in this project. I am confident that the output will be of great practical use to both Trócaire and CAFOD in charting our way as well as being of interest to all of those concerned to rise to the challenge of creating a world suffused by the Christian commitment to the dignity of each and every person.

ntroduction
Enda McDonagh, Series Editor

As part of the celebrations of the 25th anniversary of its foundation and more importantly in preparation for its work in the new millennium, Trócaire began a fresh examination of its Christian-Catholic roots. We were particularly delighted to be joined in this by our sister organisation in England and Wales CAFOD. To date three themes have been covered in this series of brief, accessible studies under the general title Christian Perspectives on Development Issues.

The aim of these studies is to set in dialogue the rich and varied Christian tradition in teaching and practice of commitment to the poor and excluded with the current concerns of development agencies like Trócaire and CAFOD. In this way it is hoped to enlighten the Christian understanding and renew the spiritual energies of Trócaire and CAFOD, and their staff at home and abroad, and of their supporters and contributors. Without such enlightenment and renewal our vision and work could become narrow and frustrating.

The first titles in the series *Human Rights, Land* and *Famine* illustrated three of the most urgent concerns for Trócaire, CAFOD and other development agencies. In seeking to expose Christian perspectives on these issues, the authors undertook a practical theological exploration from biblical background to contemporary analysis. While maintaining close communication with concrete problems of the day they have drawn on developing Christian tradition to illuminate and deepen commitment to justice in the world, that commitment element of the Gospel the 1971 Synod of Bishops called it.

Already the series launched in October 1998 has contributed towards the above objective and has been used as a resource by our partners at home and abroad. By strengthening and further exploring the ethical dimensions of our work it has enhanced our campaigning and education for justice and development. The Jubilee 2000 worldwide movement's campaign for debt cancellation which was particularly active in both Ireland and Britain has illustrated the power of bringing ethics and values into policies that otherwise risk being pursued in a self-interested way.

The series is designed not only to enhance the understanding and motivation of development agencies and workers; the studies themselves make clear how much theology has to learn from work in the field, how much theory has to gain from praxis. In fact the social encyclicals which form the basis of so much social thought and activity in the Church were themselves influenced at various times by practical developments as individual Church people and organisations reached out to the needy and excluded. In an increasingly pragmatic culture, the witness of Christian practice can be an effective way of understanding and expressing the presence of God. To do justice, the prophet Jeremiah says, is to know God. Engagement with the task of promoting a truly just world is for Christians a response to the call of the Reign or Kingdom of God. In the doing comes the understanding. Theologians need to learn by doing also and by being actively associated with the doers and seekers of justice, freedom, truth and peace.

Studies such as these will, it is hoped, prove of help to religious thinkers who have not as yet had the opportunity for more active involvement in justice issues. Being drawn into that work their insights into the whole range of Christian doctrine and practice from the Trinity, Incarnation and the last things to environmental protection will be undoubtedly enriched. Out of that enrichment they will contribute in turn to the Christian perspectives on development work that Trócaire and CAFOD are in search of here.

Multiple challenges remain. There is a whole range of particular topics and of refinements of these topics which demand parallel treatment to the benefit of Trócaire and CAFOD's work and to the benefit of theology itself. Several more of these studies are either underway or in the planning stage. These include booklets on poverty and race, gender, AIDS, and refugees. A final booklet on the theme *towards a global ethic*, which will build on the other titles in the series will draw together some key issues and reflections arising from these.

As with any studies there are some dangers in doing such a series. There is the danger that such studies might become too self-enclosing or too bland or too negatively disputatious. With a good advisory team these particular dangers have and continue to be averted. So can the more subtle one whereby the work of a development agency of explicit Christian Catholic inspiration is perceived as and/or becomes a vehicle for religious conversion.

Trócaire and CAFOD have, true to their mandate and to their genuine Christian inspiration, respected these distinctions very scrupulously. It would be very sad if their attempt to explore their theological roots were to obscure rather than clarify their integrity as development agencies devoted fully to the personal and social needs of the people they serve without any threat to the cultural or religious integrity of these people. It will therefore continue to be a matter of real concern for the editor and authors of these studies to ensure that the renewal of Christian understanding and inspiration further protects and deepens the integrity of Trócaire and CAFOD and their work. In that also they will be making a further contribution to maintaining the varied vocation and work of the whole Church in the modern world.

Executive Summary

Food is not just another commodity. Food is life. Moreover, the right to food is a fundamental one without which many other rights cannot be enjoyed. As we approach the end of this millennium it is an indictment of the international community and our common humanity that so many people do not have access to adequate food or the means to produce it.

Statistics on world hunger are to some so well known as to shed little light on the extent of human suffering: 1.3 billion people living on less than a dollar a day and over 800 million people living or existing in hunger. Put differently every 3.6 seconds someone dies of hunger and three-quarters of these are children under the age of 5. Famine and wars cause just 10% of these deaths. The majority of these deaths are from the slow grind of malnutrition, as families just cannot get enough food to stay alive. Yet the scandal remains that there is plenty of food in the world for everyone to have enough to eat. In this context the persistence of poverty and hunger are thus ultimately political and ethical challenges to us all.

Former President of Ireland and current UN High Commissioner for Human Rights, Mary Robinson, has stated that the imbalance between power and powerlessness is at the heart of the search for a global ethic. Nowhere are power imbalances more stark than in the area of food. Hence food insecurity is at the heart of the lack of a global ethic. Poverty eradication is essential to improve access to food. And because in most developing nations agriculture is the direct and indirect base for the livelihoods of the largest share of the population, agricultural policies are a vital component of integrated policies to tackle poverty.

But what of the claim that genetically modified[1] seeds with their possibilities of producing new supercrops can reduce the

---

[1] The term "genetically modified" or GM is used throughout this booklet although the corporate world at one time used "genetically engineered. Public disquiet at the concept of genetically engineered foods led to a change in language. This highlights the political nature of discussion on the subject. Corporations seeking patents look for these because they are producing something new, hence the use of the word "modification" is an obfuscation.

cost of food, increase supply and nutrition levels and thus contribute towards global food security? While technological progress may well enhance food quality and quantity over time the real question is how will those who are currently living with insufficient food fare. As power and profits are concentrated in a few agrochemical corporations controlling most of the genetically modified seed market, including those of staples such as wheat, rice and maize, crops which supply half the world's food, there is no guarantee that the poor and hungry will gain.

Nor can a technological quick fix solution to hunger be pursued without examining who controls the technology, what are its environmental impacts and indeed how does it respect the cultures of communities around the globe.

So trade policy and food security are fundamentally matters of justice and human rights. The paper draws parallels between the Great Famine in Ireland (1845-7) where dependence on one variety of potato which subsequently suffered a blight led to mass starvation and emigration with the growing dependence of global agriculture on a very limited number of crop varieties. The risks that this imposes are enormous where so many of the world's people depend on a few crops, and deserve far greater attention from policymakers than they have hitherto received.

The right to food is implicit in scripture and tradition and Catholic social teaching has made this view explicit: papal statements and social encyclicals have also emphasised that trade must benefit both parties equally. Nowhere is this more vital than in the food and agricultural trade. And Catholic social teaching in recognising the dignity of the human person, the universal purpose of God's creation, the priority of the common good and the preferential option for the poor clearly has a lot to say about food in our modern world.

Science, economics and ethics of genetically modified organisms, as well as the issue of patents and trade related property rights, need a great deal more study and a great deal less power politics. In all of this the divide in our world between developed and developing countries is evident. While many of the earth's countries which are rich in terms of biodiversity are poor and in need of external financing, there is a great risk that short-term economic transfers may press countries to accept policies that are not in the long-term interests of their citizens or indeed of an international common good. Hence the need for solidarity and vigilance as Christians who are citizens of a global family to ensure that this does not happen.

Nowhere is this more evident than in the arena of international trade and agribusiness. The answers to who benefits from indigenous discoveries and practices in agriculture and food production are to date not comforting. Indigenous communities in the developing world are being excluded from the fruits of their labour. Indeed their innovations may well cost them dearly as their assets are modified, privatised and sold back to them by agribusiness.

Meanwhile the world's top five agrochemical companies control almost the entire global genetically modified seed market. The genetic makeup of biopatented seeds is the property of corporations. And farmers' practices of saving seed for their following year's crop is a thing of the past for many patented crops. As a result of this farmers' groups in many parts of the world are calling for action against the patenting of seed varieties, which they have nurtured over generations.

The booklet in setting out the issues strives to enable each reader examine all sides of the argument about genetically modified seeds. Taking the preferential option for the poor as a cornerstone of any assessment of global food policies the conclusion is drawn that what is unethical and therefore wholly unacceptable is not the fact that research is being done that may create better crops and promote food security. But what is unacceptable and hence must be challenged is the growing concentration of control of the world's food supply in fewer and fewer corporate hands.

Taking an equity perspective, various sections of the booklet assess a range of relationships covering international decision-making structures such as the World Trade Organisation, inter-country relationships and relationships between corporations and communities. Rather than having one so-called developed versus developing world the need for a global family centred around concepts of solidarity and love of neighbour requires a radical change in our approach to food as we enter the 21st century.

CHAPTER 1

Introduction

The Importance of Food Security

Food has an integral relationship with life, for in a very real sense food is life.

It is for this reason that a struggle over food is nothing less than a matter of life and death, for food is much more than a commodity.[2] Increasingly, therefore, many are calling for a declaration that acknowledges and recognises that access to sufficient and nutritionally acceptable food be considered a fundamental human right. At the end of the Synod of 1974 the Catholic Church too underscored this importance by declaring that the right to eat is inextricably linked to the right to life.[3] This is a belief that finds a resonance in the Universal Declaration of Human Rights (1948), and in the International Covenant on Social Economic and Cultural Human Rights (1966).

Yet, every day, even as our world awakes to the marvels discovered or invented by human intelligence, we are also faced with the scandalous reality that one in seven human beings gets up to starve. In absolute numbers some 824 million people are underfed, of whom 790 million are in the developing world. Almost a quarter of the world's malnourished live in sub-Saharan Africa. As many as two-thirds are in Asia and the Pacific, 370 million in India and China alone. Within these alarming figures lies the fact that children are among the most tragic victims of hunger. While the International Food Policy Research Institute predicts a 15% decline to 135 million in the number of malnourished children under 5 between 1995-2020, 40% of all children in south Asia, and a third in sub-Saharan Africa and south-east Asia will still go hungry in

---

[2] World Food Summit commitment no.4.5, quoted in CIDSE Discussion Paper No. 22, "Food security and people's basic right to food", November 1996.
[3] cf. Giorgio Filibeck, ed., *Human Rights in the Teaching of the Church from John XXIII to John Paul II*, Libreria Editrice Vaticana, 1994, p. 228.

2020. The result will be stunted lives and stunted development.[4]

Despite laudable statements about ending world hunger the
outlook in terms of achieving food for all is bleak in spite of
resolutions like the one made at the 1996 World Food Summit
that the number of hungry people in the world would be halved
by 2015. While there are now 40 million fewer hungry people
in developing countries since the Summit, current estimates by
the UN Food and Agricultural Organisation (FAO) reveal that
the Summit's target of halving the number of malnourished by
2015 is unlikely to be met.[5]

As a publication of one of the multinational biotechnology
corporations puts it: "At the threshold of the 21st century ...
20% of the developing world's population are food insecure,
lacking economic and physical access to the food required to
lead healthy productive lives. In just one generation our world
will share the staggering demands of a population that has
doubled. ... Yet even today, without the impact of the future
population boom, farmers face many challenges to produce
enough food and fibre to meet the world's needs." [6]

Those who put forward significantly different approaches to
this problem than those offered by biotechnology companies
also recognise the immensity of the challenge. Today global
food stocks, especially publicly held stocks, are at their lowest
level for decades.[7] At the same time climatic variability linked
to global warming is making food production less predictable
than ever.

The food situation for the most marginalised in our world
today is clearly a matter of death, rather than of life. And as
history teaches us, peace cannot rest on a foundation of deep

---

[4] *The Economist*, 6-13 November 1999, page 138; see also *The State of Food
Insecurity in the World*, 1999, FAO, Rome.
[5] *The Economist*, op.cit.
[6] "Food for thought", Monsanto Enterprises, India.
[7] Devinder Sharma, "Trading food security", quoted in Advocacy Internet series,
National Centre for Advocacy Studies, Pune, India.

deprivation of the basic needs of large numbers, while others live in affluence. Today, the assets of the 3 richest people in the world are more than the combined GNP of all the 600 million people living in the LDCs (Least Developed Countries).[8] Referring to the extreme disparity that exists in the world, Pope John Paul II insisted that the "need to consider the common good of the entire family of nations is quite clearly an ethical and juridical duty".[9] Pope Paul VI had earlier cautioned us that on the overcoming of this disparity will depend "the future of the civilisation of the world."[10]

Therefore, it is part of enlightened self-interest for all, including those who are affluent, to work towards creating a world where there is food for all. To achieve this requires a type of globalisation that is built on equity, for without this globalisation can only create new threats to human security in rich and poor countries alike. As the 1991 Ministerial Declaration of the Group of 77 states: "A world divided between a rich few and large masses of the poor is unfair, inherently unstable and in the long run unsustainable".[11]

Food Security

While there are numerous definitions of food security perhaps the most useful way of summarising its key components is as follows:
Production – People have the capacity to produce the food required for a healthy life.

---

[8] UN Development Programme (UNDP), *Human Development Report 1999*, New York, Oxford University Press, p.3.
[9] Address of John Paul II on World Day of Peace, 1982, no.9; cf. Giorgio Filibeck, op.cit., p.191. "The common good retains, however a characteristic emphasis on the mutual relatedness of the concepts of person and community – the 'perfection' of one cannot take place without that of the other. It is a reminder that what each individual person has a right to expect from society is also something the individual is obliged to support society in ensuring for all its members equally." "Prosperity with a Purpose" – Irish Catholic Bishops' Conference, 1999 no.40.
[10] *Populorum Progressio*, 44.
[11] Cited in Watkins, Kevin, "Fixing the Rules", Catholic Institute for International Relations, London, 1992, p.4.

Access to food – People have access to the resources to acquire enough food through markets.
Nutrition – People have the knowledge to utilise the food available to gain the best nutritional advantage.[12]

Biodiversity and food security

Food security is also integrally linked to biodiversity. This is a term which includes the entire variety of plants, animals and other living organisms that exist on this planet. Human beings are intimately linked to this biodiversity, and not only because it is the source of our food and sustenance. Today as a result of the environmental movement we are increasingly aware of the intricate web of life that exists between humankind and all of nature. And we have gradually come to realise that the destruction of our earth's biodiversity has serious implications for us as human beings.

Currently, the extinction of various species is running at an alarming rate. As far as plants are concerned, studies predict that we will lose around 250,000 known plant species within the next fifty years. India, for example, was once home to 30,000 varieties of the one common staple, rice. Today 75% of India's rice production comes from 10 varieties. In 1949, China had 10,000 wheat varieties in use, but by the 1970s only 1,000 were still in use. Such losses are not limited to the developing world. Approximately 97% of the food plant varieties available to the farmers in the United States in the 1940s no longer exist today.[13] The spread of intensive and commercial

---

[12] See *Famine in Ireland and Overseas*, and *Famine: Causes, Prevention and Relief*, Sinéad Tynan, Trócaire, 1995; and *Hunger and Famine Today*, Sinéad Tynan, Dochas Discussion Paper, 1995.
[13] FAO Report on the State of the World's Plant Genetic Resources for Food and Agriculture, 1996, as quoted in "Erosion of Diversity" published as part of the Campaign Kit on the Ecological and Health hazards of Genetic Engineering in Foods and Agriculture, prepared by Research Foundation for Science, Technology and Ecology, New Delhi, India.

farming has contributed significantly to this mass extinction of plants and animals. This is because the farming methods followed tend to take over increasingly larger areas to grow or breed certain limited varieties of species. With this comes the inevitable destruction of commercially less profitable species. For instance, today's genetically modified (GM) crops, which follow the same intensive model of cultivation as the hybrid miracle seeds of the green revolution, are expected to jump from a cultivation area of 20 million hectares to over 800 million hectares by 2002.

The green revolution – positive and negative effects[14]

The past three decades have seen a significant increase in the number of scientifically developed high yield varieties of seed due to advances in technology. Accompanying these has been a rising trend in favour of more modern technical farming methods. Encouragement from seed companies and governments as well as the prospect of increased crop yields prompted many farmers around the globe to switch from traditional crops and farming systems to these new varieties and methods of productions.

Today, the claims made for the gene revolution echo those made for the green revolution. Hence it is useful to examine the opportunities and pitfalls which the latter gave rise to. The green revolution, launched by the FAO in the 1960s, was an ambitious programme aimed at intensifying agricultural production in response to rapid population growth and food shortages. It involved several key elements: improved varieties (especially for wheat, rice and maize) with higher yields, chemical fertilisation and irrigation, and biochemical programmes for disease, insect and weed control. At farm level farmers were offered packages of hybrid seeds, chemicals and the credit to buy these.

---

[14] Drawn from Sara Franch, "The implications of biopatenting for developing countries – Ireland's role in the review of Article 27.3b of the TRIPs Agreement", unpublished Master's in Development Studies thesis, Development Studies Centre, Dublin, 1999, pp. 60-61 and *Hunger and Famine Today* – A Discussion Paper,op.cit.

Although the green revolution undoubtedly increased agricultural productivity and food production, its consequences are highly controversial particularly in relation to its negative effects on the distribution of farmer's income and the alleviation of poverty. Its supporters emphasise the technology was scale neutral and offered a superior production system that gave higher rewards for land, capital and labour. As a result it benefited cultivators of all size farms but also landless workers through the increased labour requirements. Critics emphasised that the technology was inherently biased towards larger and more advantaged cultivators and landowners.

Furthermore, landowners benefited over tenants and labourers. Critics also stress that the green revolution's varieties of rice, maize and wheat which spread globally in a few years displaced numerous local varieties, leading to a loss of genetic diversity which in turn exposed food crops to widespread disease infestation. The increased use of agrochemcials moreover caused the pollution of natural resources and environmental degradation. Overall the green revolution represented a top-down technocratic strategy: a clear case of development from above.

Thus while in theory the green revolution was to have rid the world of hunger in practice it favoured wealthier farmers on the most fertile land while it discriminated against those who live off marginal land. Moreover, the green revolution policy has seen the redirection of resources away from crops, which form the staple diet of the poor, to crops which are likely to be exported.

While there is debate over which are the most important contributory factors to the erosion of biodiversity there is no debate over the accelerating rate at which the earth is losing its biodiversity. Over 30,000 plant species have been used over the centuries as food by humans. Today a mere 30 crops provide 95% of humanity's dietary energy.[15]

Such erosion of biodiversity has serious consequences. First of all, it threatens the long term sustainability of agriculture and the environment itself. This is simply because the fewer species

---

[15] "Erosion of Diversity" published as part of the Campaign Kit, op.cit.

available, the larger the mono-cropped areas (i.e. areas utilis-
ing a single variety of crop or seed). This situation increases
the risk of crop failures on a massive scale, since all crops of
the same variety are susceptible to the same pests or predators.
As a result, in the unforeseen situation of a blight or epidemic,
entire swathes of agricultural crops would be destroyed or
affected negatively, leading to sudden famines.. The great Irish
Famine of the mid-nineteenth century is a classic example of
this. The vulnerability created by relying on a single crop and
a single variety of that crop, the lumper potato, meant that
when the potato blight struck, the entire food source for the
majority of people was lost.

Loss of biodiversity also means that the intricate and delicate
balance between various organisms and nutrients in the environment is completely upset, the consequences of which we
are only now beginning to understand. This has led increasingly to calls for organic or ecological farming and investment
in environment friendly technologies.

At the same time farmers and scientists need a wide variety
of species to constantly innovate and create better strains of
various crops. When biodiversity is eroded the genetic material
available for innovation is reduced. After all since we humans
are nowhere near having mapped the entire DNA[16] of all living
organisms and much less create them under laboratory conditions, it would be foolish to allow and indeed to encourage the
destruction of a large percentage of our gene treasure.

A more fundamental reason for questioning this loss of biodiversity is on the grounds of respect for all life, not just of
human life. The SANFEC[17] declaration states:

South Asian communities are historically premised on the
deep sense of moral, religious and cultural values. The

---

[16] DeoxyriboNeuclic acid, i.e., the molecule in the chromosomes that encodes genetic
information and specifies its composition of proteins.
[17] South Asian Network for Food, Ecology and Culture, February 1999.

region is inhabited by multi-ethnic, multi-religious and large indigenous communities. All trees, crops, animals, birds, organisms and soils are an inalienable part of our worship, our rituals, our celebrations, our joys, our culture of sharing and our loving affinity to each other... We have a long history of spiritual and political movements (which)... have fought to preserve the integrity of Nature in her multiple expressions, including the beauty of life forms.

Pope John Paul II summarises the importance of biodiversity and our responsibility to protect it when he writes that the "moral character of development cannot exclude respect for the beings which constitute the natural world".[18] He further goes on to elaborate that we must consider the "appropriateness of acquiring a growing awareness of the fact that one cannot use with impunity the different categories of beings whether living or inanimate - animals, plants, the natural elements, - simply as one wishes, according to one's own economic needs. On the contrary, one must take into account the nature of each being and of its mutual connection in an ordered system, which is precisely the 'cosmos'." He also reminds us that since natural resources are limited, "using them as if they were inexhaustible, with absolute dominion, seriously endangers their availability not only for the present generation, but above all for generations to come." He concludes by noting that "the dominion granted to man by the Creator is not an absolute power, nor can one speak of a freedom to 'use and misuse', or to dispose of things as one pleases. The limitation imposed from the beginning by the Creator himself, and expressed symbolically by the prohibition not to 'eat of the fruit of the tree' shows clearly that when it comes to the natural world, we are subject not only to biological laws but also to moral ones which cannot be violated with impunity."

---

[18] *Sollicitudo Rei Socialis*, 34.

All these arguments are based on the belief that human beings have no right to act as despotic owners of this planet. Rather we have a duty as stewards to safeguard the environment and the tremendous diversity that is currently being destroyed by human greed and unbridled consumption.

International trade rules and food security

Food security and biodiversity are also linked directly to the rules of international trade. This connection while not always obvious can be explained as follows. In their rush towards development, a large portion of the biodiversity of the economically powerful countries has been destroyed. This means that over 90% of the earth's remaining biological diversity is in the tropical and subtropical regions of Africa, Asia and South America. The immense genetic diversity of the developing world or south has therefore become an important asset to the world economy. This obviously results in the available biodiversity becoming a source of conflict, with inevitable struggles to have control over these resources.

In this context if the market is given increasing importance, and economic criteria are used to judge disputes among nations, international trade relations will begin to play an ever more crucial role in biodiversity matters and the food security of millions. For example in the World Trade Organisation's (WTO) disputes settlement procedure, the legitimate right of countries to choose for themselves is made subservient to a trade body which decides what is best for the world market.

Thus today, globalisation is moving our world from democracy to economocracy,[19] that is from the rule of people to the rule of the market. Such an approach is often justified as being

---

[19] The term "economocracy" has been coined by the author to speak of a world order where economics or the market holds sway, and where society is therefore controlled by those with greater economic power.

more science and rule-based, and less subject to the vagaries of human ideologies. Living as we do in a culture where the alleged objectivity of science as opposed to the 'subjectivity' of religions and all ideology, is a fundamental credo of modern day society, such a plea to build an econocentric world has a distinct appeal.

With the shift to building economies and ultimately a global market economy what is of vital significance is the fact that in addition to national governments, there are a number of other key actors who are big players. Foremost among these are the multi-billion dollar transnational corporations (TNCs) whose individual net worth is often more than the national income of many countries. Indeed 50 of the world's 100 largest economies are TNCs - entities which, unlike elected govern-ments, are not responsible to anybody but their shareholders. In an econocentric world these TNCs have immense power to participate in and shape the global economy in a way that would allow them to gradually shift control of the remaining biodiversity from the forests and farms of the economically marginalised into their laboratories. Such a transfer, if success-ful, would make the marginalised even more dependent on outside sources for their livelihood and sustenance. Thus inter-national trade relations and negotiations impinge directly on the food security of millions.

This has been increasingly recognised by both developed and developing country governments as well as by many lobby groups in their respective civil societies.

For example, one of the many agreements governed by the World Trade Organisation (WTO)[20] – the Trade-Related Aspects of Intellectual Property Rights Agreement (TRIPS) - requires that

---

[20] The WTO, established on 1 January 1995 as the successor to the General Agreement on Tariffs and Trade, currently has 135 member states with a further 30 seeking to join. Unlike many other international bodies the WTO has a binding dis-putes settlement mechanism which allows countries to seek legal redress in trade disputes.

all inventions are patentable, including those based on the exploitation of biological resources. However, part of the TRIPs Agreement – Article 27.3(b) - allows WTO members to exempt plant and animals (but not micro-organisms like bacteria and viruses) from patents but still requires some form of intellectual property protection for new plant varieties. These provisions are under review and are likely be the source of much heated debate in the millennium trade round of the WTO. The WTO is fast becoming the primary venue where the battle for control of the earth's biodiversity and for food security is being fought.[21]

Taking a fully Christian perspective this battle is not merely about international trade rules. It is about a set of values. Scripture provides examples of how different world views help in understanding what is at stake. Take for example Jesus' ministry on earth. In the Sermon on the Mount, at the Last Supper and at various other moments in his ministry Jesus contrasts one view of God's kingdom (where the marginalised and the "other" get preference), with that of the then current and dominant view (where the rich and powerful and "self" claimed privilege). Such contrasts still have resonance today and lie at the core of our theological reflection on the issue of food security in our world. In pursuing trade and agricultural policies which affect food production and access we must constantly ask ourselves the question: what is better for the human race, and even for the planet that we call our home? And the decisions that we are called to make will have long lasting, even eternal consequences – affecting not only us, but millions who will come after us.

Food security, then, together with related issues of biodiversity and international trade rules, is one of the central arenas

---

[21] For a complete overview and assessment of the issues of biopatenting and food security, with particular reference to the TRIPs agreement see "The patenting of life, the poor and food security: a christian perspective on biopatenting and agriculture, CIDSE (International Co-operation for Development and Solidarity), November 1999.

where we choose or decide our future – either to learn to live together with all of creation, or to be torn apart as a planet.

CHAPTER 2

From the worldview of the gene giants[22]

Faced with the alarming and scandalous fact, that one in seven human beings is struggling for food today, the emerging gene giants have put themselves forward as providers of a realistic solution to the problem of world hunger. As Monsanto, one of the five largest gene giants, writes in one of its publications: "There are just two ways to increase food production - put more land under cultivation or increase yields."[23] Since putting more land under cultivation would mean the destruction of the already scarce forests and sanctuaries of our planet, they claim that the only realistic alternative humanity now has is to boost yields on available land. This will require great creativity, enormous intellectual effort and unprecedented co-operation between research institutions, public and private, and the many different sectors that contribute to food production. A significant but not the only answer may lie in agricultural biotechnology, which is likely to play a crucial role in expanding agricultural productivity in the 21st century.[24]

Genetically modified crops are at the cutting edge of applied research in the wonderland of biotechnology. Advocates of the life-science companies[25] propose that such crops should be allowed to play their due role in bringing about food security.[26] These life science TNCs have already

---

[22] The gene giants are those extremely TNCs who through a series of mergers are increasingly controlling the food-related genetic research in the world today. They are also known as the life sciences companies, a new terminology to collectively describe businesses that use biology as a common platform technology for all their products in life-related fields like agriculture, nutrition and medicines.

[23] "Food for Thought", op.cit., p.5.

[24] Ibid.

[25] cf footnote 21.

[26] Moreover, other ways of improving food security such as better access to food and better distribution are not given such high priority under such an approach.

invested huge sums of money in research and experimentation with the genetic material of plants and animals, and even of humans, with the expressed aim of finding new products that would open larger and more lucrative markets to them.

What are genetically modified (GM) crops?

For centuries farmers have been interbreeding strains of the same species (e.g. rice) in order to get better varieties of that particular crop. While this was done for generations within local communities, the hybrid seeds that kick-started the green revolution in a number of countries were the result of more focused and planned efforts, where seeds from various locations, even different countries, were interbred in more controlled conditions to give rise to better combinations. However, even this more efficient method had its drawbacks. This was because scientists and farmers were never quite sure what exactly to expect from a combination of two or more seeds, since they had to wait for the seeds to actually germinate and produce, before they knew what traits would finally be included in the new seeds.

This same process was given a huge boost once scientists came to recognise the importance of DNA within every living organism, and even more when they were able to relate the qualities of a living organism to specific strands of DNA. Once they could recognise these connections and isolate particular DNA strands, the next step, which was logically and successfully followed, was for scientists to cut and paste suitable DNA from one plant or seed onto another. Thus, with greater precision, they could give rise to a new seed/plant variety that had the precise qualities that were desired.

The result of studies of the DNA of various living organisms led to the ability to put them together in newer combinations, even those that could never be found in nature. Thus animal genes have been intermingled with plant genes,[27] and there are endless possibilities of similar cut and paste operations using genes from plants, animals and even human beings.[28]

With this technology increasingly being refined and utilised, scientists were and are able to create what we today call genetically modified crops, i.e. seeds/crops which can be created for specific purposes and conditions. The gene giants propose that their research may allow the human race to overcome the dangers that arise from the unpredictability of food production.

Advantages of GM crops

Biotechnology does indeed have the potential to improve crop yields, reduce chemical usage, improve food quality and remain environmentally friendly. A look at the introduction of hybrid seeds and other advanced farming techniques in the production of crops in a country like India for example, during the green revolution, shows that food production rose from 50 million tonnes a year in 1950 to over 200 million tonnes a year for the last several years. As a result food production has kept pace with and even overtaken the rate of population growth. Thus India has attained self-sufficiency for a considerable period of time.[29] The new biotechnology techniques (leading to genetically modified crops) can be seen as creating even more powerful tools for obtaining manifold increases in food production. Or put differently, this gene revolution may be far more radical and far-reaching in its impacts that the earlier green one.

---

[27] This has been termed the verminator technology as it can include the genes of rats in seeds.
[28] The Harvard oncomouse is an example of this genetic crossing between species. See Oscar B. Zamorra, "Genetic engineering and intellectual property rights: moral and ethical issues", p.3.
[29] "Food for Thought", op.cit., p.11.

From a food security viewpoint such a gene revolution could have immense benefits. For example plants could be engineered to survive in hostile conditions (e.g. water scarcity areas) by splicing onto them the genes of those weeds/crops that have, over centuries of tending by humans or through simple evolution, developed the ability to survive in such environments. Similarly, seeds can be engineered to be resistant to particular pests, thus reducing the need for labour intensive care of such crops. Or crops can be developed that take the most suitable qualities from a variety of genes to create new super-crops. Scientists could also engineer crops that have much longer shelf-lives, leading to a saving of huge quantities that are often lost in storage or in transportation.[30] The possibilities, as can be seen from these few examples, are limitless, especially since this technology is not limited to introducing genes from plants alone, but can introduce animal and human DNA to get certain desired products.

Response to some concerns regarding GM crops

Increased risk and unknown food and health impacts
A criticism that has been levelled against GM crops and seeds is that they will be much costlier and will therefore be of little use to improve the food security of the poor farmer. Life sciences companies respond by claiming that such higher costs will be more than recovered by farmers from the increased output they will get. Moreover, these companies point out that because the seeds are engineered for specific conditions farmers will need to spend less on other agricultural inputs like labour, pesticides, chemicals etc.

In responding to concerns regarding the health hazards of such GM crops, the companies argue that genetic

---

[30] Although it is worth noting that poor roads and a lack of basic storage for food crops in impoverished areas are responsible for much of the food losses that hurt the food insecure.

experimentation means that they know much more about the new creations than farmers or scientists would ever know about new crops that they breed in traditional ways. As a result extensive tests can be carried out to make sure that the new crops are as safe as possible. Thus the companies argue that GM technology actually lessens the dangers of new crops creating unforeseen health hazards.

As far as the question of the unintended long term effects of tampering with nature that genetic modification necessarily involves, the companies admit that this will not be known except after a considerable period of time and extensive field trials. However, they contend that the introduction of any GM seeds or other products will only happen after they have fulfilled all the requirements laid down by the various regulatory bodies in the respective countries in which they are operating.[31] They could also claim that a look at the history of medical research has shown that the advantages of introducing new products far outweigh the few cases where over time new products have shown such negative effects that they have resulted in the product being withdrawn.

A recent conference which debated the ethical questions raised by such research concluded: "The application of genetic modification to crops has the potential to bring about significant benefits, such as improved nutrition, enhanced pest resistance, increased yields and new products such as vaccines. [Therefore] the moral imperative for making GM crops readily and economically available to developing countries who want them is compelling".[32]

---

[31] There are of course serious questions being raised about the effectiveness of these regulatory bodies. While in some countries these bodies are not yet established, in others like in Britain, there are questions regarding their independence since the members of the companies being regulated, like Zeneca, also have their representation on these committees. Cf. Simms, Andrew, *Selling Suicide: Farming, False Promises and Genetic Engineering in Developing Countries*, Christian Aid, 1999, p.4.
[32] Nuffield Council on Bioethics, Executive Summary, p.2.

Corporate v. farmers' or community property rights

Such innovation, the companies claim, can only be in the best interest of the human race, since the responsible use of this technology will enhance the food security of millions. Furthermore, they argue that the pursuit of knowledge can never be artificially stopped by rules and regulations. Once human beings have discovered, or begun to discover the wonders of biotechnology, there is no way that the genie can be put back into the bottle. Any attempt to do so by ill-conceived laws under the guise of ethics or allegedly national interests will only serve to push the knowledge underground. And from there it will surface in even more virulent forms in the hands of those who would have little scruple in using it to further their own nefarious ends.

Moreover, the development of this technology requires much investment of time, talent and material resources - an investment that these companies would not be likely to make if there was no possibility of reward. Consequently, in order to safeguard what they see as their legitimate rights, these TNCs have lobbied governments and international bodies with the huge resources at their command in order to ensure that intellectual property rights (IPRs) are made to apply all over the world. Their goal is that markets will be completely opened to their products. This will allow them to expand the sales of their products without individual governments interfering on grounds of national policy or for other reasons that go against what they call free market conditions. Thus they argue for market-rule-based international trade agreements that are applicable all over the world.

Until such rules are applicable and enforceable all over the world, the companies involved in such research believe that their rights will not be safeguarded adequately. Therefore, they have at times used their research findings to develop biological weapons to defend their property rights. As a result "every gene giant multinational has patented or admits it is working on genetically sterilised or chemically dependent seed."[33] A few examples of the direction in which such research is going can be seen in the following.

a) *Monsanto's terminator seeds:*[34] Efforts are underway to introduce into GM seeds traits that would ensure that crops produced from such seeds will not have any viable seeds that can be used again. This means that farmers will not be able to use seeds from their own crops to plant in the next year. Instead they will have to invest in new seeds every year.

b) *Astra Zeneca's Lazarus-type seeds:*[35] Here the crop that is produced will give the farmer new seeds that can be re-used again. However, such seeds will lie dormant until certain genes are activated by a special chemical. In this way the company does not need to spend on stocking up on the seeds, as this will be the responsibility of the farmer, but will only have to make available chemical inputs which are easier to stock and transport without deterioration.

c) *Novartis' genetically mutilated seeds:*[36] In this type of seed the natural plant functions which help the crop to fight disease are consciously disabled or regulated, such that they can regain these abilities only on the application of a particular chemical treatment that the company also provides.

These are only three examples of the various biological methods being used by the life sciences companies to ensure what they consider their legitimate property rights are safeguarded for the requisite period of time of the patents i.e. 17 to 20 years. - by which time they hope to recover their investment and make handsome profits.

---

[33] Rural Advancement Foundation International (RAFI) News Release, 29 March 1999 in "Traitor technology: damaged goods from the gene giants".

[34] Ibid.

[35] Ibid.

[36] Ibid.

The approach of the gene giants is based on the assumption that food insecurity is primarily seen as a problem of lack of adequate production. Indeed many from the corporate world and other international bodies focus on the growth of food production as the primary engine to food security. Furthermore, these gene giants argue that the necessary increase in food production will only be possible if those who have the economic strength and resources are allowed the freedom to pursue their own ends, for not only would they profit, but the benefits would trickle down to the hungry.

This world view is very attractive to those who are not hungry or marginalised, for it is a perspective where the powerful retain their position of pre-eminence and decide what is in the best interests of those without power and without food. It is significantly different from the approach to power and wealth in scripture, notably at the last supper where the master becomes servant, where the first must be last.

CHAPTER 3
From the viewpoint of the hungry and marginalised

A Christian perspective – the preferential option for the poor

All reflections, theological or otherwise, depend crucially on one's starting point. At the same time the possibility of finding a starting point that is universally acceptable is becoming less and less likely. Today Christians cannot assume that everybody shares their own values (even Christians disagree among themselves). Neither, can Christians assume that their own approach is so perfect that they have nothing to learn from others. In the Catholic Church at least, our exposure to other religions and our openness to learn from them, especially since Vatican II, have challenged such myopic opinions in many parts of the world.

This is not to say that there are no values that are shared by the majority of human beings. In fact the Universal Declaration of Human Rights, and the International Covenants on Civil and Political, and on Economic, Social and Cultural Rights, provide a set of values which a significant portion of the human race regards as valid. And common values can also be identified across religions and political analyses. For example the gospel of Jesus, enriched by Catholic social teaching shares values with the talisman of Gandhi,[37] the insights of indigenous peoples on our living relationship with nature, the harmony of the yin-yang espoused by the Daoist, the demand for detachment in the Hindu/Buddhist way of life, the complete submission to God that Islam stresses, and even the insights on structural injustice that Marxism has given us in our recent past. All these insights can help us find our way through the complex

---

[37] The talisman of Gandhi is nothing else than the face of the poorest man. Gandhi taught that one could decide on the ethics of one's action if every decision was made keeping before one the face of the poorest man.

questions that confront us as we pilgrimage to the kingdom that Jesus came to herald, where we all – not just the powerful and the successful - shall have life, and have it to the full.

It is crucial, therefore, that any theological reflection must begin with an openly articulated perspective. The previous chapter incorporates a perspective that, consciously or unconsciously, exists in many of our own lives, where the winner is one who defeats others, where the successful have much power over others, and where altruism is about giving from one's excess to others in need.

The perspective that informs the remaining reflections in this paper flows from our understanding that the pre-eminent law of the Gospel is the love of neighbour, and in the carrying out of this law there must be a preferential option for the poor and the marginalised. This priority option for the marginalised is an essential element of Catholic social teaching. Thus Pope John Paul II, in his encyclical *Sollicitudo Rei Socialis*, writes that we must identify ourselves not with the rich man, but with Lazarus the beggar who used to sit at his gates.[38]

In this context it is preferable to use the word equity rather than social justice, not because there is anything wrong per se with the latter term but because of a particular flavour which has come to be associated with the latter. After all words tend to slip and slide and change as they are used and overused, and the term social justice has come to have connotations of the rights only of the poor and not those of the affluent, rights that we must try to *give* to the poor. This connotation (though certainly not present in the true meaning of the term social justice) seems to create an atmosphere of reverse discrimination that many secretly rebel against. It also continues to keep the disadvantaged in the position of supplicants.

Equity on the other hand has the connotation of each getting his or her fair share. For example we do not speak of social

---

[38] *Sollicitudo Rei Socialis*, 42 and *Centessimus Annus*, 39.

justice when our house is burgled and we demand our goods back. We speak of justice or equity that our goods be returned to us. Equity therefore has a less antagonistic ring to it, since everybody, rich or poor has a right to what is legitimately theirs. The catch, of course, is in deciding what rightfully belongs to each.

Keeping this perspective in mind, we can begin to reflect on the questions that arise as we explore the question of food security today. As mentioned earlier there is the question of equity in the matter of food for all, in the realm of knowledge, and in international negotiations. There is the question of equity among nations and between the rich and the poor. In this context there is also the question of judging equitably between private (individual or corporate) rights and community rights, and which takes precedence, and in what circumstances. At the same time there is the issue of our relationship to life as expressed in the immense biodiversity that our planet possesses. What is or rather what ought to be our relationship with nature; what control can we rightfully wield over other living beings; or when and to what extent can we tamper with nature and life?

Though all these aspects can be reflected upon from various starting points, this reflection is clearly based on the starting point of a preference for the marginalised. It is this point of departure that will guide us first of all in posing the question: Do we really have too little food?

Looking at the causes of food insecurity

The basic contention of the biotechnology industry is that the hunger of millions today is primarily due to the lack of available food. Is this true? Have human beings been unable to produce enough to feed our world's burgeoning population or are the roots of world hunger to be found elsewhere?

One estimate indicates that the world produces enough grain to provide every human being on the planet with 3,500 calories a day. This estimate does not take into account many other commonly eaten foods such as vegetables, beans, nuts, root crops, fruits, grass-fed animals and fish. When all foods are considered together there is enough to provide at least 43 pounds of food per person per day.[39] In 1997 an American Association for the Advancement of Science study revealed that 78% of all malnourished children under five in the developing world live in countries with food surpluses.[40] It has also been pointed out that the world's food production has outstripped population growth by about 16% over the last 35 years.[41]

Yet history has shown that famines recur or that even without acute famine situations, many go to bed starving. We must ask ourselves what is the cause of such hunger which is an affront to our common humanity. The answer for many is that such outcomes are the result of wrong political choices rather than the absence of food. The great Famine in Ireland in the mid-19th century is a stark example, though not the only one. Over one million Irish people died in this famine which was at its height in the period 1845-1847. About 2 million others emigrated. Yet during these same years Ireland remained a net exporter of food. Surely then the hunger that drove so many to destruction was perhaps caused more by wrong political choices than by scarcity?

Professor Amartya Sen in his research on famines in Bangladesh, India, Ethiopia and in other parts of sub-Saharan Africa shows that other factors such as poverty and the price of food rather than food supply factors are the prime causes of famine.[42] People are shocked to discover that during the Ethiopian famine of 1984, that country was using some of its best farming land to grow animal feed for export to Britain and

---

[39] Quoted in "Myths about world hunger dispelled", in Dr. Peter Rosset, *World Hunger – Twelve Myths*, Advocacy Internet, NCAS publications,1999.
[40] Ibid.
[41] Ibid.
[42] Simms, Andrew, op. cit., p.2.

the rest of Europe. Again, for example, in 1995, India exported five million tonnes of rice, and $625 million worth of wheat
and flour. At the same time more than one in five Indians went
hungry.[43]

The role of human choice can also be seen in non-famine
situations. Thus, for example, in Costa Rica while beef production doubled in 14 years, the beef consumption of the local
population decreased from 30 pounds to 19 pounds per person. This increase in production was used to service foreign
consumers.[44] This same scenario is present in a number of
countries where the international market, and not the needs of
the hungry in these very countries, determines the types of
crops that the farmers produce. Such trends have led Amartya
Sen to conclude that "hunger is the inevitable outcome of the
normal workings of a market economy."[45]

Pope John Paul II in his speech to the 28th FAO Assembly
in 1995 sounded a similar note when he said: "Hunger and
malnutrition are the result of perverse mechanisms inherent in
economic structures, or are the result of unjust criteria in the
distribution of resources and production, of policies established
with the aim of safeguarding the interests of particular groups
or various forms of protectionism."

What is clear from all this is that food insecurity can never
be explained by population density and a resultant inadequacy
of food stocks. Instead people are hungry because they lack
resources to access food through the cash economy. Taking
this latter view it is clear that concentrating on new technology
to increase food production will not adequately address the
political and structural dimensions of food production and distribution. Poverty and powerlessness must also be tackled.
Despite this, powerful countries and corporate bodies have

---

[43] "Food? Health? Hope?" a GRAIN publication, p.2.
[44] Ibid.
[45] Ibid.

manipulated the media and the public discourse, so that for most people population control, increased food production and the further freeing up of market forces are seen as the three keys to solving hunger.

These three perceived solutions have one key thing in common – they do not demand any change in power relationships between the powerful and the powerless or put differently between the affluent and the hungry.

Looking at a biotechnology solution to food insecurity

But what of the argument that while an inadequate food supply is not the problem today, it could be a problem in the future as the amount of buffer food stocks declines? And as it can be argued that for better or worse genetically modified crops are here to stay, then if we do need to explore ways of increasing food production is this the best route to this end?

The use of biotechnology will not necessarily mean a very significant increase in overall food production as compared to ecological or organic farms. In comparing ecological farms with chemical intensive farms,[46] it was found that the former were just as productive and profitable. Therefore fostering such ecological farms would have no negative impact on food security. Additionally such farms have the added advantage of reducing soil erosion and the depletion of soil fertility while greatly lessening dependence on external inputs.[47] Other studies indicate that, as far as the gross output per unit of land is concerned, small farms often outdo large ones. And in comparison to GM crops, research on Indian farming showed that land reform and simple irrigation boosted crop yields by 50%, compared to 10% for GM crops. [48]

---

[46] Myths about world hunger dispelled", op.cit.; see also Christian Aid reports, "Selling Suicide", op.cit., p 2.

[47] Ibid.

[48] John Vidal, "Christian Aid calls for 5-year freeze", The Guardian 10 May 1999.

Furthermore the use of such technology, by the admission of its own advocates, tends to minimise employment. This has direct implications for food security, because if people are starving in spite of food being available, then it can only mean that they do not have the resources to buy/access the food. The hungry need income through increased employment if they are to have enough food. Thus attempts to minimise employment would only exacerbate the food insecurity of the most vulnerable.

Other effects of this technology on a large scale can be seen in its effects on insects and other organisms. Some applications make plants resistant to certain insects by making them produce their own insecticides. But widespread use of these insecticides could mean that the resistance of these insects to the pesticides will gradually increase. If the emergence of such resistance is rapid, not only will farmers in such countries face crop failures having become completely dependent on GM crops, but they will also give rise to super insects which can be only overcome by more and more toxic insecticides.

GM crops also have other environmental impacts on the food chain. For example when this technology is used to change the flowering time of plants this affects the breeding period and habitat of insects and this has knock-on effects throughout the food web. Similarly the special insecticides used with GM crops are quite likely to have a domino effect on other beneficial insects which feed on these pests which have eaten the toxins from the doctored plants. This too would seriously affect the food web.

And of course there is an even greater degree of uncertainty concerning the outputs of biotechnology, as once new seed varieties are released into nature, it is impossible both to turn back the clock and to accurately predict the risks and full consequences of their use. This is particularly true with regard to the introduction of genes across species, since such combinations could never be found in nature. Thus, potatoes have been engineered with genes of the silk moth, chicken, viruses and bacteria; tomatoes with those of the flounder fish; and tobacco plants with genes from the Chinese hamster.[49]

Taking all three issues together it would seem that while the use of biotechnology in food production does have value in expanding the frontiers of human knowledge, it is not a viable route as far as food security for the millions who are under-nourished and starving in our world.

Food security for the world's hungry demands decentralising control over production while biotechnology centralises control. Food security demands a move towards non-chemical production so that farmers are less dependent on external inputs and their environment is protected. Biotechnology firms in contrast, are consciously moving towards chemical dependency. And food security demands increasing employment opportunities for the marginalised (so that the hungry have resources to access food), while biotechnology is moving us towards lower levels of employment and higher prices for agricultural inputs.

Equity in international relationships and food security

If the true cause of food insecurity is to be found in human choices that place economic efficiency over equity, we need to look at international and national agreements/policies to see whether we are serious about working towards the elimination of food insecurity in our world today and in the future.

---

[49] Christian Aid report, "Selling Suicide", op.cit. Besides the unpredictability of such combinations, there is also the ethical question whether it is right for us to tamper with species in such a way that we might end up creating monstrosities like human animals who could be used as beasts of burden or killing machines. Unfortunately this booklet has not been able to delve into this ethical aspect as the focus is on food security.

International trade in agriculture occurs within the framework of the General Agreement on Tariffs and Trade (GATT) and its successor the World Trade Organisation (WTO). While much discussion about the international trading system centres on reducing agricultural protection and creating a free exchange of these products so that the benefits of trade are accessible to all countries, the reality of trade is much different. Developing countries, much of whose populations rely on agriculture for their livelihoods, continue to lose out. In 1950 they accounted for half of all agricultural trade. Today their share of this trade is down to one quarter.

These trading disadvantages are compounded by economic liberalisation measures which mean that most developing countries are unable to invest in the research, infrastructure or processing facilities necessary to develop their agriculture. As a result economic power in this field is being concentrated in the hands of a few multinationals, which between them control most of the world's private seed supply and agricultural inputs.

That is why the United Nations Development Programme in its latest *Human Development Report* states :

> Competitive markets may be the best guarantee of efficiency, but not necessarily of equity.... When the market goes too far in dominating social and political outcomes, the opportunities and rewards of globalisation are spread unequally and inequitably - concentrating power and wealth in a select group of people, nations and corporations, marginalizing the others. ... When the profit motives of market players get out of hand they challenge people's ethics - and sacrifice respect for justice and human rights.[50]

A former Secretary General of the WTO reflected a similar view when he admitted: "In reality the multilateral trade system is an

---

[50] *Human Development Report, 1999*, op.cit., p.2.

engine for growth, but not for distribution, because world trade can solve the problem of increasing resources only, but these are later distributed at international, national and regional levels - this is the duty of other policies which have nothing in common with the commercial system."[51] This was echoed in *Populorum Progressio* which said that "industrial initiative alone and the mere free play of competition could never assure successful development."[52]

It is clear that access to food, and not just better crops (even if potentially possible) is essential for greater food security for those who starve. Thus free trade which pits large corporations against smallholder agriculture as if they are economic equals, and where the former increasingly dominate food and agricultural markets will clearly be inadequate in ensuring food for those who need it most. Market intervention in developing countries is also geared towards supporting more commercial farmers and export crops.[53] If one accepts that hunger is political, then a globalisation process which is not based on equity will take us nowhere close to overcoming the food insecurity our world faces today.

This means, that at the very least "we have to ensure that access to the basis of food security does not pass from government control to corporate control".[54] *Octogesima Adveniens* warns about this when it states: "Under the driving force of new systems of production, national frontiers are breaking down, and we can see new economic powers emerging, the multinational enterprises, which by the concentration and flexibility of their means can conduct autonomous strategies which are largely independent of the national political powers, and

[51] Renato Ruggiero, former Secretary General of WTO, February 1996, quoted in CIDSE "Food security and people's basic right to food" , p.6.
[52] *Populorum Progressio*, 22.
[53] Devinder Sharma, "Trading Food Security", Advocacy Internet, February 1999, NCAS, Pune, India.
[54] VOICE (Voice of Irish Concern for the Environment) Position Paper on the Revision of Art. 27.3(b) of the Trips Agreement.

therefore not subject to control from the point of view of the common good. By extending their activities, these private organisations can lead to new and abusive forms of economic domination on the social, cultural and even political levels."[55]

It is for this reason that many development agencies are convinced that GM crops have the potential to create the classic preconditions for hunger and famine. This is because these technologies inevitably mean that the ownership of resources gets concentrated in too few hands - a result inherent in farming based on patented proprietary products. For example, today 80% of patents on GM foods are owned by only 13 TNCs and biopatents threaten the livelihoods of 1.4 billion farmers in the developing world who currently depend on saved seeds for the following year's crop. In addition to this the global food supply is gradually getting narrowed down to a very limited number of crop varieties which are widely planted, and which, as has been pointed out earlier, open up possibilities of sudden famine situations.

Thus both these elements contribute to creating the worst-case scenario as far as food security is concerned:

a) dependence on a few varieties of crops, which in turn can easily lead to the dangers of mono-cropping mentioned earlier; and

b) the marginalisation of the hungry, as even these varieties are patented and hence controlled by economically powerful bodies whose primary aim is the creation of profit.

It should also be remembered that while control by governments who are democratically elected is certainly a better option than control by companies who are accountable to no one but their shareholders, the agricultural policies of many governments indicate that government control or intervention is not always a good solution. For within many governments

---

[55] *Octogesima Adveniens*, 44.

there are local elites who manage to oppress their own. Would the solution then be to allow the means and facilities for food production to remain primarily in the hands of the local poor, especially women? The United Nations Development Programme in various reports has shown how the empowerment of women in marginalised families (e.g. through increases in her income) invariably leads to the entire family receiving tangible benefits.

But such a gender-based approach requires a Copernican revolution in our world view, for it is not only patriarchy that is being challenged here, but our very understanding of power. In Christian terminology what we are really asking is that the meek should be allowed to inherit the earth and its fruits, that the last should be first.

Equity in the context of respect for other viewpoints

Equity also demands respect for different viewpoints – especially those of the less powerful. Failure to do this inevitably means giving in to a new kind of "imperialism and hegemony", which Pope John Paul II warns would occur if we do not work towards a "real international system …which will rest on the foundation of the equality of all peoples, and on the necessary respect for their legitimate differences."[56]

Particularly with regard to relationships between the strong and the weak, this respect is crucial, for in such relationships even freedom can become a dangerous tool used to subdue the marginalised under the guise of apparent equality. Pope John Paul II pointed this out when he quoted Lacordiare: "Between the strong and the weak, it is freedom which oppresses and law which sets free". [57] For when two unequal parties sit together to negotiate, complete freedom for each

---

[56] *Sollicitudo Rei Socialis*, 39.
[57] Address to the ILO, 1969.

one to take as much as possible inevitably means that the weak will come out second best from the encounter. Leo XIII noted this a long time ago when he wrote: "if the position of the contracting parties are too unequal, the consent of the parties does not suffice to guarantee the justice of their contract for freedom of trade is fair only if it is subject to the demands of social justice."[58]

This aspect of equity takes on great importance when we come to deal with the contentious question of property rights, especially intellectual property rights (IPRs) which play a crucial role in the global marketplace. IPR was first raised as a multilateral trade issue in 1986 as a means of cracking down on counterfeit goods. Today these rights have been extended into the field of biotechnology and living organisms through TRIPs.

What are patents?

Like other forms of intellectual property rights such as copyright and trademarks, patents are a form of incentive and reward for inventions. They are designed to encourage commercial innovations, while allowing the knowledge behind them to be shared. If the knowledge of an invention were free for anyone to exploit commercially, the inventor would want to keep it secret, to protect it. There would be little economic incentive to share the knowledge. Thus patents give inventors a temporary monopoly over new inventions from which they can economically benefit, in return for publishing information about the invention. In this way, inventions do not die with the inventor, and others can try to invent something better, but different enough not to infringe the claim of the original patent.

Intellectual property (IP) systems were thus designed with a view to the common social good, balancing the interests of producers with those of users of intellectual works. To be

[58] Pope Paul VI in *Populorum Progressio*, 59.

patentable, an invention, either a product or a process, must be:

- non-obvious for someone skilled in the art, i.e. not simply be an extension of something that already exists but require an inventive step;
- novel, i.e. not previously known;
- industrially applicable (or useful) in some way.

A patent right lasts for a fixed time period (20 years minimum under the TRIPS Agreement, which is a long period given the pace of technological change) after which anyone can use the invention. The precise terms applying to patents vary from country to country and patents only apply in the country/ries in which they are granted.[59]

However, as a matter of respect for different cultures, equity demands that the right of peoples to apply their own approach to their own collective property must be respected. Pope John Paul II confirms this when he states that "not even the need for development can be used as an excuse for imposing on others".[60] If this is taken seriously, then it must be remembered that for many cultures, especially among indigenous communities, the knowledge that they share is collective and intergenerational. This means that no one, not even their own members, and certainly not their governments can sell or transfer the ownership of these resources to anyone else, for they hold it in trust for their communities, both present and future. In their eyes, "traditional knowledge of the natural environment is by nature collective - based on the free exchange of knowledge and biodiversity. In contrast intellectual property rights of any kind are by definition a limitation of this knowledge flow and collective nature, and thus are against the very nature of this kind of knowledge, its development and even its survival".[61]

---

[59] The Patenting of Life, the Poor and Food Security, op.cit.
[60] *Sollicitudo Rei Socialis*, 32.
[61] "The European Patent Directive : License to Plunder" GRAIN publication, January 1999.

What are bio-patents?

IPRs have traditionally been associated with industrialised and market-based economies. Until the development of commercial plant breeding, they were little used in agriculture, as innovation largely resulted from farmers freely sharing seeds and inter-bred animals to produce a wide range of varieties and breeds suitable for differing climatic conditions.

Moreover, until 1970, discoveries in nature could not be patented, even if the inventor found some synthetic way to make the same product, which merited being called an invention instead of a discovery. Since 1970, this distinction has been gradually eroded, under economic and scientific pressure to allow living organisms and their parts, and biological processes to be patented as inventions in some countries. Genetic engineering is now providing radically new ways to manipulate biological resources, giving rise to new industrial processes of immense economic value. In principle, genes can now be exchanged among plants, animals and micro-organisms regardless of their sexual compatibility.

Companies engaged in biotechnology have therefore pressed for the adaptation of classical intellectual property law to cover life forms, as being no different from any other form of technology. One reason is because, unlike chemicals, living organisms can reproduce themselves after they have been sold. This limits the potential profitability of biological inventions for anyone who seeks to appropriate them or monopolise their use and sale. Demanding patents on plant varieties thus became an obvious option for those companies who wished to protect the revenues that such new technology promised.

In the USA, limited patents on some plant varieties were first allowed in 1930. In 1980, as modern biotechnology began to shape the development of intellectual property law, the US Supreme Court ruled that a genetically-engineered oil-eating micro-organism could be patented. In 1985, the US Patent and Trademark Office allowed genetically-engineered plants, seeds and plant tissue to be patented. They extended this ruling to animals in 1987 by allowing a patent on a mouse genetically engineered to develop cancer. This move toward patenting life forms or biopatenting has more recently been mirrored in Japan and in the European Union (EU).

Patents and other forms of IPRs (such as plant breeder rights which were developed in Europe as a less rigorous alternative to plant patents) will affect the future of global food security. Control of plants and animals through patents will strongly influence who controls the food system.

Yet it is precisely here that equity is not present. For today the biodiversity that has been amassed in communities over centuries is gradually being spirited away by the life science companies and other researchers. Subsequently these resources are patented, and the plant, the gene and the knowledge, which had belonged to a community for generations, suddenly becomes the property of economically powerful corporations or individuals.

The demand from these corporations and individuals, supported by their powerful governments, is that these newly acquired property rights be safeguarded through patents all over the world. Into the bargain the price of resources which were once easily accessible to the economically disadvantaged has increased dramatically. Such biopiracy not only extends to plants but also to the genes of human beings.

Examples of biopatents

In 1995 there were 29 foreign patents drawn from the neem tree in India, - a tree whose insecticidal properties had been well known by local communities and used by them for millennia. As a result the price of the neem seed has grown from 300 to 8,000 rupees (or approximately £6 to £160) per tonne in 20 years. In the Amazon a US citizen gathered an ayahuasca plant from a garden and then patented it under US law, turning it into an important asset for the US based International Plant Medicine Corporation. Ayahuasca is considered to be sacred in many Amazonian cultures, and is used in important traditional healing and visionary rituals. In

Cameroon a casual visitor from the University of Wisconsin picked up a plant that produces brazzein, the protein that makes their j'oublie plant so sweet, and then patented this in the US and in Europe. The university now claims this researcher is the sole inventor of this potentially very lucrative sweetener. Subsequently the university has gone on to genetically engineer bacteria to produce brazzein, meaning that Cameroon villagers will definitely be excluded from any commercial development of the sweetener that they have nurtured over the centuries. Such biopiracy is not restricted to the economically weaker countries. Australian public agricultural research institutes have claimed plant breeders' rights over six traditional pasture varieties from Sardinia in Italy.[62]

Human genes too have not been excluded from these efforts to gain profitable patents. Patents on a cell line of a 26 year old woman of the Guayami community in Panama, and similar patents for cell lines taken from the Hagahai people of New Guinea and from certain Solomon Islanders, all have been the subject of patent claims - some of which were subsequently refused only because of an international outcry.[63] On the other hand a US citizen, John Moore, had his sick spleen patented by the doctor who operated on him and the courts in the USA upheld the patent.[64] By the end of 1997 the European Patent Office had received at least 102 patent applications on human genes, proteins, cell lines or products thereof, while worldwide there are at least 394 such applications.[65]

This differential understanding of what can or cannot be patented, what can belong to individuals and what belongs eternally to the community, meant that "until recent times patenting laws differed from country to country reflecting the way in which different cultures and political systems weighed up

---

[62] CIDSE Discussion Paper No. 22, "Food security and people's basic right to food", November 1996.
[63] Ibid.
[64] Ibid.
[65] Ibid.

the often conflicting claims between compensating the inventor and ensuring that the public benefits from the new product. The pendulum normally tilted in favour of making information and innovations available that would benefit the whole society rather than securing the private interest of the inventor. Most Third World countries, for example, refused to recognise patents on food and medicine and other basic products that are deemed basic human needs. Earlier patent agreements like the 1883 Paris Convention and the 1886 Berne Convention (updated in 1946) recognised that individual countries had particular needs and priorities and that these would be reflected in national patent legislation".[66]

But such differentiated laws were not deemed to be suitable by those who saw a huge market in these patents. As a result "the first break with these country-specific patent laws took place during the Uruguay Round of the General Agreement on Tariffs and Trade (GATT) which was concluded in 1994. Under pressure from its corporate sector the US and other northern countries pushed for harmonisation in the law affecting intellectual property rights across the world."[67]

But as those fighting against the control of the gene giants claim: "The problem with TRIPs is that the only inventions it recognises are those that meet the criteria of novelty, inventiveness, and industrial applicability or usefulness".[68] As a result

> this system of rights denies property rights to local and indigenous knowledge, practice and innovations. TRIPs only recognises as worthy of protection inventions that conform to the northern definition… Rights are recognised only when they generate profits and are capable of industrial applications. …Local people end up being exploited and made

---

[66] Quoted in Sean McDonagh, "The Scramble to Patent Life", Columbans, London, 1999.

[67] Ibid.

[68] Taken from Bio-IPR docserver, "Southern African Development Community (SADC) workshop on TRIPs" March 1999.

even poorer by developed countries because their knowledge is accessed freely, then 'treated' in laboratories in the north, and ownership rights claimed through patents. Royalties are then paid to new owners by those who make use of the patented products.[69]

The UNDP further underscored these concerns. It has listed four characteristics as implicit to international property rights. These are: a stress on private rights as opposed to common rights; recognition of knowledge and innovation only when they generate profits, not when they meet social needs; innovation in a formal setting rather than embodiment of indigenous knowledge, and acknowledgement of an international rather than a domestic and local use perspective.[70]

It is clear then that in their very basic concept, these IPRs are loaded against the interest of the poor and marginalised, and consequently pay scant respect to the rights of indigenous people. Furthermore they also ignore cultural diversity in the way innovations are created and shared, as well as diverse views on what can and should be owned, from plant varieties to human life. As a result there is a legal theft of centuries of knowledge from some of the poorest countries to the richer ones, and particularly to the laboratories of TNCs.

Under such an approach an equity perspective is lost as the views of certain economic actors and cultures take precedence over other cultural viewpoints. If this inequitable situation is allowed to develop further the hungry will become even more marginalised in the realm of knowledge since strictly enforced property rights of this sort will raise the price of technology transfer, even as it simultaneously pirates away the knowledge resources of developing countries. From the perspective of the hungry, in a knowledge intensive and inequitable global economy, the future looks bleak.

---

[69] Ibid.
[70] As reported in Christian Aid, *Selling Suicide*: "Food and genetic engineering", op. cit.

From a theological point of view, this question of property rights has been an issue that the Church has struggled with for centuries, since what we face here is a tension between private (individual and corporate) rights and community rights. Historically, the Church, has often defended the right of private property, even speaking of differences in society as being divinely ordained.[71] This was one of the main reasons that religion was called the opium of the people, as it was perceived to be a system that kept people quiescent in the face of inequality in society.

And yet there was the other strain of Church teaching that also existed and which stressed the rights of the community over private rights. Thus, the early Church community voluntarily chose to share their personal property so that no one would be in want. Years later Aquinas would lay down conditions for ownership of property, insisting that "the common purpose of the goods of creation overrides legal dispositions when it comes to the urgent need of people".[72] During the Famine in Ireland, the Irish bishops did speak out on the subsidiarity of the rights of private property to the common good.[73] In recent times Pope Paul VI accepted that the poor have the right to take what they need for their sustenance, notwithstanding any rights to property that others may hold, when he wrote: "God intended the earth and all it contains for the care of every human being ... All other rights whatsoever, including those of property and free commerce are to be subordinate to this principle".[74] The Brazilian bishops also echoed some of these almost lost strains when they asserted: "It is lawful for a man to succour his own needs by means of another's property by taking either openly or secretly".[75]

---

[71] Christian Perspectives on Development Issues, *Land*, Denis Carroll , Trócaire, Veritas, Cafod, 1998, p. 48.
[72] Ibid, p. 47.
[73] Ibid, p. 49.
[74] *Populorum Progressio*, 22.
[75] Carroll, op. cit., p. 48.

Thus the Church, in its more prophetic moments, was able to question the right to private property when it impinged on the good of the community. Since private property rights are subordinate to the community's rights, it is a matter of equity that one must give back to communities what is rightfully theirs. In the light of Church teaching on the injustice inherent in contracts between the strong and weak, it may be pointed out that even property that is legally taken away can still be unjustly taken. Put simply what is legal is not always just and what is just is not always legal. It is when we look at the situation from this perspective that the injustice in international relationships is most evident.

"It is estimated that three-quarters of the plants that promote active ingredients for prescription drugs came to the attention of researchers because of their use in traditional medicine. The current world drugs/medicines market for medicinal plants derived from leads given by indigenous and local communities is estimated at $43 billion. In addition the value to the international seed industry of the crop varieties improved by traditional farmers is estimated to be $15 billion".[76] As if this were not enough other national products developed by indigenous people and local communities include sweeteners, perfumes, fabrics and cosmetics. These applications, too, are expected to grow in commercial use, leading to huge profits for a tiny minority and nothing for the communities from whence their original resources came.[77]

Furthermore, very often the decisions about what to cut and paste come from the knowledge of local innovators.[78] But what patent holders or companies do is to expropriate such knowledge from the true innovators and transfer it to themselves by treating it in a laboratory . "The belief is that what comes out of the rain forest of Ecuador or a farmer's field in

---

[76] BIO-IPR docserver " Press statement on regional workshop of SADC.

[77] Ibid.

[78] "The European patent directive: license to plunder", GRAIN, 13 January 1999.

Sri Lanka is 'natural' and unpolished, while what comes out of a lab in Palo Alto is a 'product of science' and should be patented as an invention".[79] This privatisation of collective knowledge has been termed biopiracy. As a result, centuries of tending and selection of seed by communities is given no reward or acknowledgement, whereas the one who builds on this inherited knowledge, and adds one small step to the process is allowed by such property rights systems weighted in their favour to become the legal owner of all this cumulative knowledge. Thus when developed country governments insist that the lack of effective intellectual property rights means the loss of billions of dollars of revenue that they have a right to, they are significantly distorting the truth.[80]

If equity is taken seriously, then it is no more a matter of helping the needy that is at stake here, but that the countries and companies which have robbed the economically poor of their intellectual property, should give back what they have stolen. As Sean McDonagh writes: "When we realise that much of US agriculture was developed from plants and genetic resources freely imported from other countries, then the question of justice or equity would demand that the US should repay its 'genetic debt' to the world".[81]

The fact that nobody seriously believes such countries or TNCs will repay such debts is not surprising. After all this robbery is only a more sophisticated repetition of what happened during the period of colonisation all over the world. Britain,

---

[79] Ibid.
[80] RAFI estimates that US agricultural chemical royalty losses (in the terms adopted by US researchers in a 1990 study of US negotiating positions) are approximately US$202 million. Pharmaceutical losses are approximately US$2,545 million. On the other hand estimation of losses from the non-payment of royalties for farmers' folkseed varieties was US$302 million and for products derived from medicinal plants amounted to approximately US$5,097 million. Thus developing countries are net losers to industrialised countries. Data taken from TRIPS and Biodiversity by Gurdial Singh Nijar, published by Third World Network, p. 33.
[81] cf. Sean McDonagh op. cit.

for instance, has never compensated its former colonies for the immeasurable harm it has done to them to strengthen its own economic base. The Opium Wars were another instance where Britain used its military might to force China to accept payment in opium for its imports from that country. These were clearly cases where equity was not practised, and the present regime of biopiracy follows the same pattern. That is why *Evangelii Nuntiandi* points out that the sufferings of people, including those caused by "injustices in international relations and especially in commercial exchanges" are "situations of economic and cultural neo-colonialism, sometimes as cruel as the old political colonialism".[82]

Cultural neo-colonialism (i.e. imposition of one culture on another) is also seen today in the matter of the patenting of life. Human beings, particularly those brought up in the ethos of the semitic religions, have generally seen themselves as the crown of creation and have been given the rest of creation to take care of and use as the need arises. This stewardship aspect has been repeatedly affirmed Catholic social teaching down the ages: "It is a requirement of our human dignity, and therefore, a serious responsibility, to exercise dominion over creation in such a way that it truly serves the human family. Exploitation of the riches of nature must take place according to criteria that take into account not only the immediate needs of people, but also the needs of future generations. In this way, stewardship over nature entrusted by God to man will not be guided by short sighted or selfish pursuit; rather it will take into account the fact that all created goods are directed to the good of all humanity."[83]

The eastern traditions and indigenous thought patterns offer a more holistic understanding of nature. "They have recognised that each organism or species including human

---

[82] *Evangelii Nuntiandi*, 30.
[83] Pope John Paul II's Address at the United Nations Centre, Nairobi, 2; cf. Human Rights Teaching in the Church, op. cit., pp. 218-219.

beings is inextricably related to the environment and ultimately depends on the whole ecosystem for their survival."[84] In that sense these other traditions do not see human beings as higher, but only as part of the larger harmony of nature. In either case, however, there is a call to nurture nature.

In contrast to these approaches the new IPR regime outlined above seeks to promote a view of life as a commodity. This system goes against a holistic view of life, and forces the culture of an economically dominant group on the rest of the world. Life, in almost all the religions and cultures of the world has always been treated with reverence and awe as a gift of God. However the biotechnology route towards IPRs moves us in the direction of seeing life only as a collection of genes and chemicals that can be manipulated, bought and sold, by those who happen to have the economic resources to be the first to take out a patent on them. Furthermore it could well mean that within a few decades "the entire human genome... would be owned by a handful of companies and governments"[85] Such a view on the patenting of life forms thus accords with most cultures and ethical traditions which make a clear distinction between animate and inanimate objects. A Christian perspective would certainly insist that nothing should blur that distinction – and certainly not the desire of individuals or corporations or governments to control the earth and our food. For the earth and all that lives belongs to the Lord.[86]

The US Supreme Court decision which ratified the right in that country to patent life apparently shared the same market view of life, when it stated that the "relevant distinction was

---

[84] "The European patent directive", op. cit.

[85] Sean McDonagh, op. cit. In this context the Human Genome Organistion Project (HUGO) deserves some mention. HUGO is an informal consortium of universitites in North Amercia, Europe along with corporate organisations, funded by the US National Institute of Health, which aims to sample fifteen thousand endangered human communities and patent their genes.

[86] Psalm 24.

not between living and inanimate things" but whether living products could be seen as "human-made inventions".[87] Andrew Kimbrell in his book *The Human Body Shop* considers that the US Supreme Court's decision to allow the patenting of life forms,[88] has "transformed the status of the biotic community from a common heritage of the earth to the private preserve of researchers and industry".[89] He fears that the ruling has "set the stage for increasing competition among multinationals as they vie for ownership and control of the planet's gene pool, patenting everything that lives, breathes, and moves".[90]

There are also other objections to the patenting of life forms. It is argued that the geneticist or biotechnologist does not create genes, cells or organisms *de novo*. They identify, isolate and modify these entities which is a very different operation from creating them. Thus an identification or even re-arrangement of living organisms or parts of living organisms should hardly constitute a monopolistic right over the organisms themselves.

The Church of Scotland clearly stated its opposition to the patenting of living organisms on these grounds when it commented:

> Living organisms themselves should ... not be patentable, whether genetically modified or not. It is wrong in principle. An animal, plant or micro-organism owes its creation ultimately to God, not human endeavour. It cannot be interpreted as an invention or a process, in the normal sense of either word. It has a life of its own, which inanimate matter does not. In genetic engineering, moreover, only a tiny fraction of the makeup of the organism can be said to be a product of

---

87 Quoted in Sean McDonagh, op.cit.
88 Ibid.
89 Ibid.
90 Ibid.

the scientists. The organism is still essentially a living entity, not an invention. ... It may take much intellectual effort to decipher a gene and identify its function, but the gene is just as much a discovery of nature as the animal. Despite the considerable investment involved, the identification of the gene's function is not an ethical ground to claim exclusive rights. Even though intellectual effort has been used, it is of the nature of discovery not of invention.[91]

Taking this approach, accepting the patenting of life forms would lead to a situation that keeps the poor dependent on the rich even in the matter of life. As the Latin American Declaration on Transgenic Organisms states :

Genetic engineering is a technology driven by commercial interest. It is not necessary. It forces us to become dependent on TNCs which control it, putting our autonomy to make decisions about production systems and food security in real danger. Especially in the field of agriculture, there are traditional and alternative technologies which do not pose such risks and which are compatible with the conservation of biodiversity.[92]

The legitimate fear is that over time such a "patenting scramble will remove many life forms from the domain of the commons where they have provided many services for humans and other creatures. Under a patenting regime these life forms will now become the private property of northern transnational corporations. Life will only have value in so far as it generates a profitable return on investment for large companies."[93]

[91] Church of Scotland, *Supplementary Reports to the General Assembly and Deliverances of the General Assembly 1997*, May 1997.
[92] Quoted in Sean McDonagh, op. cit.
[93] Ibid.

Equity with regard to human knowledge

While biobiopiracy and biopatenting clearly play a part in restricting the rights of the human race as a whole to the fruits of knowledge, there are also those who argue that patent laws also hinder progress in science.

This shift towards the privatisation and secretive control of huge areas of scientific knowledge is already happening through the granting of extremely broad patents. For example, the US company Agracetus, now owned by Monsanto, applied for a patent that covers all cotton seeds and plants which contain recombinant gene construction. Other companies were so alarmed that the issuing of a number of such broadly defined patents would give enormous control of staple food and other commercially valuable plants to a few corporations that they filed objections to the Agracetus patent at the US Patent and Trademark Office.[94] Other wide ranging patents awarded in the USA include a patent for "all genetically engineered cotton products", "all genetically engineered soya bean", "all T-cells of Guayami (Panama) women" and 4000 human DNA and gene fragments.[95] Those who cloned Dolly the sheep have applied for a patent that would give them exclusive rights over all cloned animals.[96] These kinds of broad patents are frightening when one realises the power they hand over to individuals and corporations at the expense of the rest of the human race.

As a result, opponents of patenting are concerned that such a patenting culture will promote a climate that hinders the normal exchange of information that is essential in order to promote scientific research. The scientific information and the materials that are required for research will become more expensive and difficult to obtain if one corporation owns a patent on the material. This in practice will deter rather than

[94] Ibid.
[95] See Box 5 in Oscar Zamora, op. cit.
[96] Quoted in Sean McDonagh, op. cit.

promote research. A research culture focused on patenting will also mean that scientific research will no longer be undertaken simply to increase our understanding of the world, to search for truth or to promote the public interest. It appears that scientific research in genetics is driven by the search for corporate profit rather than by a concern for human or planetary well-being. It is interesting that, in the mid-1800s, the parent company of what later became Ciba-Geigy (which in turn later merged with Sandoz to form Novartis, the second largest seed corporation in the world, and one that was awarded the third largest number of biotechnology patents in the US between 1980 and 1993) fought attempts to establish patenting laws in Switzerland. There is a modern ring to their arguments. They claimed that "patent protection forms a stumbling block for the development of trade and industry... The patent system is a playground for plundering patent agents and lawyers."[97]

The similarity between what happened with the Enclosure Acts in Britain in the 18th century, and what is happening today with trade-related intellectual property legislation, has not been lost on commentators. Pat Roy Mooney of the Rural Advancement Foundation International (RAFI) points out:

> rich landlords who orchestrated the enclosure movement... argued that the commons must be privatised so that they could take advantage of the new agricultural technologies and feed growing urban populations... In the same way and with the same arguments as the Enclosure Acts used to drive rural societies from their ancestral lands (and rights) TNCs are now pursuing another Enclosure Act - the intellectual property system –to privatise the intellectual commons and monopolise new technologies based on these commons. The Landlords have become the Mind Lords. In the post-

---

[97] Ibid.

GATT world of new biotechnologies, these are also the Life Lords "[98]

And though biotechnology firms and the governments that support them claim that patents will foster research, both UNCTAD (1996) and the World Bank (1998) themselves have pointed out that there is little systematic evidence linking foreign direct investment inflows or increased research and development with strong patent protection.[99]

Equity with regard to the sovereignty of nations

If, indeed biopatenting poses a threat to food security and even the food sovereignty of nations, one could ask why developing countries would sign various WTO agreements such as TRIPS, when these would allegedly put them in such a disadvantageous situation.

One of the most crucial reasons is the fact that although developing country governments have come to realise that the trade rules are not really in their favour, they may have also concluded that not to play ball would marginalise them even further in our increasingly global economy. Many may regard opting out as committing national economic suicide especially when they negotiate with the same developed country governments on aid and debt issues.

Thus Christian Aid in a position paper in 1993 said: "In general the Uruguay Round will make worse the terms on which many will trade with the rest of the world. But if the Round will not conclude and a trade war will burst out among the great occidental blocks, poor countries will be taken in a crossfire and they will incur even worse losses".[100] All this

---

[98] Ibid.
[99] VOICE (Voice of Irish Concern for the Environment), "Position paper on the revision of art 27.3(b) of the TRIPs Agreement", July 1999.
[100] A position paper prepared by Christian Aid in 1993 for the Ecumenical Council of Churches.

means that changing trade rules is not a neutral technical process, but actually a jockeying for power. As a result governments "traded concessions in one area for others in a different area."[101] And as power relationships play a major role in the drafting and signing of various international agreements, the quad of the EU, USA, Canada and Japan can often impose their will on weaker countries as they see fit.

The instance of the francophone countries of Africa signing a UPOV[102] type agreement on patents in 1999, after they were led to believe that such a monopoly mechanism would bring West African countries into the biotech world of the 21st century and that it would be their best option to comply with the mandatory requirements of the World Trade Organisation, is a good example of this power. It was only when they were suddenly confronted by a tremendous reaction from the other members of the Organisation of African Unity (of which they themselves are members) that they began to realise that they had contradicted their own agreement of just the previous year which they had signed with 62 other heads of African governments. Only then did they realise that there were other options more suited to African interests

---

[101] WTO and Food Security – an ActionAid position paper.
[102] The UPOV (International Union for the Protection of New Varieties of Plants) was adopted in 1961 and since revised in 1972, 1978 and 1991. The UPOV system of Plant Breeders Rights (PBRs) is a *sui generis* (unique or specific to a country) system However it was developed for institutional, commercialised breeding in developed countries in which farmers have to pay royalties on such seed, and may not suit all countries. Only varieties that are distinct, uniform and stable are eligible for "protection" under UPOV. Widespread use of such plants in developing countries has led to genetic erosion and has reduced biodiversity. More than 75% of agricultural crop varieties and more than 50% of domestic livestock breeds have disappeared from farmers' fields in the last century. According to the International Plant Genetic Resources Institute (IPGRI), a system suitable for intensive, industrialised farming systems is unlikely to be suitable or appropriate where there is a lot of subsistence farming. This is true in many developing countries and various governments are developing national legislation for protecting plant varieties appropriate to their situation. However, this is a challenging time-consuming task requiring resources.

which they could have followed in fulfilling their obligations under the GATT.[103]

It is also clear in hindsight that differential access to information and funds for preparation also meant that the final document establishing the WTO was weighted against the poorer countries because the latter were not able to prepare as thoroughly for it as they would have if they had the resources. These stark difference can be seen in the fact that the US representative Carla Hills came with 400 advisors, a number that exceeded the entire contingent from the continent of Africa. Even the daily functioning of the WTO is weighted against these poor countries, as can be seen from the fact that many of them, 29 least developed countries, cannot afford permanent representation in Geneva where the WTO has its headquarters. This has serious implications, for though the WTO system works on consensus, the system also stipulates that the positions of countries will not be accepted by phone or fax.[104] This is compounded by the fact that meetings are held simultaneously at different venues on a variety of issues, and the small number of representatives from poorer countries, even when they do attend, can obviously only attend a fraction of the meetings that are relevant to their interests.[105] All this seems even more ominous when we realise that by signing the WTO agreement disputes between countries are now subject to decisions made by an appointed trade body which will decide purely from the perspective of what is good for the market.

Turning in particular, to the patenting of life forms, it is clear that the wording used in Article 27.3(b) of the TRIPs agreement was a carefully negotiated compromise, reflecting not only the differing interests and conflicts among the industrialised countries, (including differences between the US and the

---

[103] "TRIPs, Traps or Dice? A series of articles on TRIPs and Agriculture", RAFI, July/August 1999
[104] VOICE, op. cit., p.11.
[105] WTO and Food Security.

EU and between the European Commission which negotiates on the EU's behalf, its member states and the European Parliament), but also the differences between developing and developed countries. It was in fact the European Commission negotiators who persuaded developing countries to accept the current wording, pointing out that the legislation within the EU did not allow such patents. However, since the time that document was signed the EU has passed its own biopatenting directive. As a result the EU has now changed its stance and has joined hands with the US to prevent a full-scale review of the provisions of Article 27.3(b).[106]

Behind the WTO/GATT negotiations was the presence of some major transnational gene giants who were keen to make sure that the rules were made so that they could benefit. As these companies are mostly located in the north, it is no wonder that their own governments strongly supported their position. Many of these corporations have a financial strength that is more than that of many countries, with the result that they can bring tremendous pressure to bear on politicians at both national and international levels. This influence is quite obvious for those who wish to see it. For example, Donald Amstutz, the senior US negotiator on agriculture until 1987, was a former president of Continental Grains. Similarly Cargill Corporation, the world's largest grain trader, assumed responsibility for preparing the US negotiating papers in preparation for some of the earlier rounds of trade talks on agricultural issues.[107]

[106] BIO-IPR docserver "TRIPs Council discusses plant patenting" 26 April 1999.
[107] Kevin Watkins, op. cit., p. 38. Similarly "former US Trade representative, Mickey Kantor, is on Monsanto's board, and former Deputy US Trade representative, Rufus Yerxa, became the firm's chief international trade lawyer (headquartered in Brussels) in April 1998. Cf. "Biotechnology's takeover of the seed industry", IPR Info No. 23 – Revised, published by Institute for Agriculture and Trade Policy, USA.

Equity with regard to individual choices on food security

One can also ask why would farmers buy such seed if it is detrimental to their sustainability? Aren't they free to do as they wish? An answer to this can be found in the fact that companies interested in this field of biotechnology are beginning to merge into ever larger corporations which control greater chunks of world seed production. At the same time public sector plant breeders are rapidly diminishing in size and numbers. "In 1996, 24 of an estimated 1,500 seed companies controlled 50% of commercial seed production, and a year later just 10 controlled 40% of the same production".[108] The process of mergers is also taking place in allied fields that impinge directly on the agricultural world and therefore on food security. "By 1998 the top 10 companies in pesticides controlled 85% of a $31 billion global market.... In 1993 just 10 countries accounted for 84% of global research and development expenditures and controlled 95% of the US patents of the past two decades. Moreover, more than 80% of patents granted in developing countries belong to residents of industrial countries."[109]

It can be expected that such rapid corporate consolidation in the seed sector may well result in fewer seeds being available, as these mega-companies create virtual monopolies. Under such a scenario farmers will be left with no option but to buy these companies' seeds. And when there is a similar consolidation in allied sectors, e.g. agrochemicals, the power of these companies to control production is further increased.

This move from public to private control of seed markets is happening all over. In Thailand, private companies play more of a role in seed production, with the Government simply overseeing distribution.[110] In Brazil, Monsanto has spent

[108] "Biotechnology's takeover of the seed industry", op. cit.
[109] Human Development Report, 1999, op. cit.
[110] ActionAid paper, "Astra Zeneca and its genetic research", 1999.

more than $1 billion in buying seed companies and is plan-
ning a $550 million factory to produce pesticide compatible
with its GM soya crops. In India it has big holdings in the
country's largest seed company and has invested more than
$20 million in the country's leading science institution. It has
also paid more than $1 billion for the international seed
operations of Cargill, the world's largest private grain sales
company.[111]

Added to this is the increasing control over research that is
coming into the grasp of a few TNCs. For example in India
many local scientists may well prefer to work at Monsanto's
genomic research centre in Bangalore which offers higher
salaries and better conditions than Indian Government laboratories. Worldwide a number of publicly funded research institutions have been bought by or have made research agreements
with TNCs. Thus, for example, Zeneca has made a £50 million investment as part of a ten year collaboration with the
John Innes Research Institute in the UK.[112] As research institutions accept funding from private companies, national public
sector plant breeding programmes relevant to poor farmers
may be undermined, may gradually be deemed unnecessary
and as a result be denied adequate resources. Is it perhaps
for this reason that the US Department of Agriculture which has
a 5% share in one version of the terminator gene is confident
that it will be so widely adopted that farmers will only be able
to buy seeds that cannot be re-germinated?[113]

The use of pesticides is a good example of how large companies gradually influence farmer behaviour. Moreover, given
these companies' control over seeds the possibility of farmers
reverting to older methods may not arise anymore as once

---

[111] "Selling Suicide", op. cit.
[112] "Astra Zeneca and its genetic research", op. cit. It has also been pointed out that
Monsanto has donated US$23.5 million to Washington University, and Hoechst built
an entire US$70 million biotech research laboratory for the Massachusetts General
Hospital, where research on crop genetics is also being conducted.
[113] "Selling Suicide", op. cit., p. 3.

farmers' own seeds are neglected they are eventually completely lost to them.

Even government aid programmes to farmers in developing countries, funded as they are by rich donor nations, are often tied up with help to buy these newer seeds in the same way that the green revolution was fostered. Thus if governments choose to support the development of GM seeds or as will be the case in many poor countries, they are unable to offer continued financial support to their public sector seed supplies the result will be that the farmers will be left with little or no choice. "The alternative exchange outlets which benefit small farmers such as farmers' markets, seed exchanges, etc. may be undermined as they receive less funding and other encouragement from governments."[114] And so as seed saving becomes more and more difficult, seed will increasingly be purchased from these TNCs which have a stake in keeping the farmer dependent on their products. As a campaign statement puts it among some NGO groups in India: "When saving and reusing saved seed becomes a crime; when corporations calling themselves life sciences corporations start to deliberately extinguish life; then life itself is being colonised".[115]

Another method used by these gene giants is the entry they are attempting to make through established NGOs in a country. In Thailand Monsanto offered micro-credit schemes to farmers through IRRI (International Rice Research Institute), PDA (the Population and Community Development Association) and the Department of Agriculture. Under these schemes conservation tillage will be used. This is described as the "practice of substituting the judicious use of herbicides for mechanical tillage".[116] Thus the project aims to change Thai rice farming practices in ways which would suit Monsanto's technology and its future financial interests since such farms would become

[114] "Astra Zeneca and its genetic research", op. cit., p. 12.
[115] BIJA Satyagraha, loosely translated "The truth campaign in the matter of seeds".
[116] "Monsanto in Thai micro-credit project", 9 April 1999.

highly dependent on the products of multinational companies. Similarly in 1998 Monsanto offered the Grameen Bank of Bangladesh $150,000 to provide loans to poor farmers to buy Monsanto's agricultural products. After vociferous protests Grameen withdrew.[117]

Thus through the use of international pressure, marketing techniques, inadequate or one-sided information, gradual monopolisation of seed stocks into the hands of a few companies, government support and even apparently philanthropic efforts, farmers are drawn into a situation where there is little chance for them to continue to use their own seeds, even if it is in their future interests to do so. Farmers thus are strongly guided into "freely" choosing such products.

And so while powerful countries vociferously advocate political rights of the individual, the market surreptitiously takes away the rights of the marginalised and hungry to choose freely the kind of food they will grow

---

[117] Sara Franch, unpublished thesis, p. 56.

Concluding Reflections

CHAPTER 4

The perspective outlined in this booklet is one in which the love of neighbour is the starting point, with a preferential love of the marginalised being at its core. Jesus' ministry was all about lifting burdens. "Whether the burdens were created by a scrupulously strict religious sensibility or blind obedience or political corruption or grinding poverty or sickness or lack of self-esteem or pride or prejudice, the result was the same: people were in need of healing".[118] And therefore the call of Christian discipleship is that we always seek to lift burdens. This call is particularly relevant as we approach the Jubilee year of 2000, for in the Judaic tradition the jubilee was the year when all debts were cancelled.[119]

Looking at the issue of food and food security from the perspective of the preferential option for the poor, we are led to the conclusion that what is unethical and therefore unacceptable is not the fact that research is being done that could perhaps create better crops and assist in the food security of the world. What is unacceptable is that control of the world's food supply is concentrated in fewer and fewer hands. It is also an affront to our common humanity that nearly one in seven people is hungry while there is enough food in the world to meet everyone's needs.

What is unethical is the inequitable relationship between nations and peoples that finds particular expression in international agreements. What is also unethical is the investment of huge resources in a GM path to achieve food security, which from the viewpoint of the marginalised is only likely to make them even more impoverished and hungry. What is unethical

---

[118] Christian Perspectives on Development Issues, *Famine*, Michael Drumm, pg 39, Trócaire, Veritas, Cafod, 1998, p. 39.
[119] The term "jubilee" comes from the Jewish teaching that every fifty years, all debts were cancelled, and all those who had become slaves because of unpaid debts were set free.

is also the lack of equity in the systems that are in place both in terms of regulating research on these matters and in terms of the distribution of the fruits of human knowledge, particularly as these are so intimately related to the future of our human race and the planet. And finally, what is unethical is to attempt to take control and to monopolise living organisms in complete disregard of the cultures and sensitivities of numerous cultures which revere life.

Moreover, this entire reflection also leads us to challenge areas of our own lives. We live in a world where the rights of the individual have been seen as essential to our world view and suddenly we are reminded by Catholic social teaching that "above the particular common good of a nation, the common good of the entire family of nations is quite clearly an ethical and juridical duty."[120] (World Day of Peace 1986) Reflecting then, on the issue of food it is clear that communities and the human race have rights that must take precedence over individual or corporate rights.

We live in a world where making profit through competition is seen as an ethical way of making a living as long as one keeps within the law. Yet the teaching of the Church has warned that human competition is such that it "ever compromises and violates peace"[121] (World Day of Peace, 1969). Thus suddenly we are forced to ask whether what we have traditionally considered as legal (and therefore presumably ethical) ways of making money, when expanded into the new fields of biotechnology may not be moral anymore, and whether there is a type of profit making that is unethical in itself?

In such a situation Christians have a double task before them. In order to be able to make sense of this reality. Christians must learn to look once again at Jesus, not just at his words but at his whole story, and try to find out how it

[120] Giorgio Filbeck, op. cit., p. 150.
[121] Giorgio Filbeck, op. cit., p. 186.

relates to one's own personal story today. And there is another task, for to look properly at one's own personal story one must also be willing and open to look at the influences that affect us, whether they be from other religious or non-religious sources. Only then will the Christian be able to find out what the Spirit of God is calling us to do today. Thus the gospel of Jesus, enriched by Catholic social teaching and the insights of those other traditions and ideologies that consciously choose to keep the marginalised to the forefront, can help us find our way through the complex questions that confront us as we pilgrimage to the kingdom that Jesus came to herald. A kingdom where we shall all have life, and have it to the full.

The debate on the causes and solutions to hunger in our world will not go away. But what is clear from this reflection is that unless a pro-poor ethical perspective informs those who set policies on food and new technologies, the outcome is likely to be more hunger rather than less as we enter the 21st century.